# THE ABSOLUTE LETTER

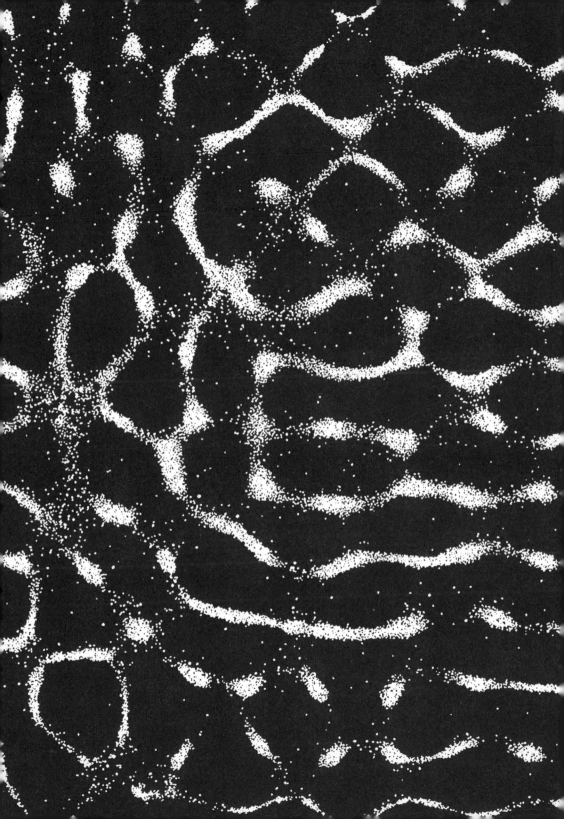

ANDREW JORON

THE

# *ABSOLUTE LETTER*

FLOOD EDITIONS

CHICAGO

Copyright © 2017 by Andrew Joron
All rights reserved
Published by Flood Editions
www.floodeditions.com
ISBN 978-0-9981695-0-7
Design and composition by Quemadura
Printed on acid-free, recycled paper
in the United States of America
Versions of poems in this collection have
appeared in the following publications:
*Armed Cell, Aufgabe, Cloud Rodeo,*
*Colorado Review, BAX: Best American*
*Experimental Writing, The Elephants,*
*Fourteen Hills, Hambone, Lana Turner,*
*The Nation, New American Writing,*
*Pallaksch. Pallaksch, PoetryNow* (Poetry
Foundation), *The Volta,* and *X-Peri.*

TO ROSE

WHO KNOWS WHO

IS A BELL.

## THE ARGUMENT; OR, MY NOVALIS

According to the German Romantic poet Novalis, verbal language is a subset of what he called the "general N-language of music." The very letters of the alphabet, in his eyes, dissolved into vibrational patterns: "Figurations of sound waves like *letters*," he wrote in his philosophical notebooks (1798). "The letters originally must have been *acoustical figures. A priori letters?*"

Novalis was provoked into thinking about "sound writing itself" by the German physicist Ernst Chladni's book *Discoveries in the Theory of Sound*, published in 1787. The book describes how Chladni scattered flour or sand on glass or metal plates, then stroked the plates with a violin bow: as the plates resonated, forcefield-like patterns appeared in the particles on their surfaces. For Novalis, these "figurations of sound waves" were the "a priori letters" of a universal script.

The world itself is composed of the letters of the Absolute: anything, real or ideal, that undergoes a self-complicating—ultimately musical—form of motion becomes a sign of the processual emergence of the Infinite within the finite.

# THE ABSOLUTE LETTER

# *FIRST*

If nothing comes first
    —there will be a Riot of time.

Over over-
Throw
    there is nothing.

A, ad-
    vance, a
Threat
    of dark upon
    light, the very Idea
    of color.

Unred
    the road, its
Turn a-
Part
    —its pattern
    a

    connective void, the
Unlikely a-

Voidance of all
    rays, of all right.

So hopeless is the play of Place,
    canted to one & one condition, shun.

    Now to speak the spike
Into unhurt name, the
    heart—

That thought of *that*, that
    thought of thought
    alone—

# THE ABSOLUTE LETTER

Proof primitive:

That two sticks
    point toward
A
    vanishing:
A
    accumulation.

Compass-mouth
    stopped by its own measure:

    that, belated, uncalculated, yet
Shone as shown:

A
    version in in-
    version.

    A
    pure statistic, imperative to stay
Past saying—

for
*ever* fails
Before *every*, son & sun.

A
    bent intent.
A
    atom:

Meaning *word*, missing a
    letter, waits upon a power within a powder.

All in thrall
    to what thrives
    as *there*, & its theory—

    as throw & throw, as mantic
Tick through unmeant Time.

Fallen letter, avian V, in-
    verse A.

Two parallels meeting at

A
Road eroded to a line—
A
    dark abstract stroke.

# ILLOCUTIONARY REELS

- Die rolls, rules die.
- Reaper, repairer, here appear.

- Wear sorrow, noiseware.
- Ring, bring news from nowhere.

- Offering fearing, Law of the Father, both neither & nether beard.
- So motion drips down: first & last liquid.

- Voice voice, mark mark, as *voices of ice* is to *vices of eyes*.
- For a chorus is incarcerated in every point of space.

- Every sentence repeats the past.
- "Senseless" alone tunes tense to the height of heat.

- Arc as ark hides hives, swarming in relation to the rest of reason.
- The circle of time is an arc hive.

- Language lies like a block on the tongue.
- So, called, passion, so, cold, position.

- To know no now.
- The animal leaves its senses every moon, every moan. No-man, gnomon.

- *We be*, betrayed: *we* to treat the trait of *alone*.
- *House* has *roof* to refer to *fire*.


- Written rotten: the later the letter, the righter the writer.
- Think, thank, thunk: O god-dawn, gone down.


- Enough of knife, of knife, of of.
- & the wound so wound, the sound so wound.

# BREATH'S BREAKS: TEN TAKES

*To the ghost of Barbara Guest*


1.


Next to nothing, touch is
    the chill
    torch of this instant, its senseless
Exterior.

*Why*'s its own
    winterward
Cause—that lowering
    ascent's
Tensing of the Laws, as
    a sentencing

From the cold frieze of Time.
No freer ear—

Drop direct, heir of here.
Drape ape.

2.

Red planet, planned
Eternity.

*Le vide, la vida*—
    a/version of/to
The retailed tale.

One & two, the very Plus
    of want—all
      secluded in the solar cloud.

Light, follow
    I, fantastic stick.

3.

C defines the speed of the deeps.
(See *elsewhere*.)

First, eternity waits (for time to begin).
No bigger web for that fly (now flown).

Too wise, I whisper spare whys two ways:
That one is the way of the other.

Utter utter night, such sibilant syllable—
Each tear, each tear, entire.

See over C: that absolute is blinding
Black & white at once.

Say O for C: the rhyme
Of eye & symmetry fails. Try I, then tree.

## 4.

Slow train coming.
Trace low
    slumming: the owed code, the
    *must* of dead dust.

Shake, cash: too-tiny
    machineries
    of the blood
    blare through, throw
    the mind.

Solo so low, so
    low as silence.

**5.**

A fecund fakery
    of void is *black*'s equivalence, as is
    *white*'s of quaver.

To show is to
    show a shower of opposites, the One
    shapeless place.

The dark of light
    tries its intricacies
    even here, in the hold of cold, the tolled.

6 .

Wish before want, unearthly ethic.

First one body explodes, then another.
There is no explanation.

Where is spring followed by winter?

How to read the
    unwhole, the
    red spread of a landscape of skin?

**7.**

Spilled / blued / spelled / blade.

Later open
Up letter:
    thy "thine" sign, thy
Mine
Of meaning.

Once relented, in runnels, to
Writing, my *blued* was
    read:
    Own blown.

8.

Careless care, so
Fall-
    ful, the

    start of art. Stop
    step, step
Stop.

Is then
    all *starred*, all
    *stored* of heart, bell, in-
Curable core?

Half
    laugh:
    a mental lament.

## 9.

Sempiternal the parts—all their
    pattern & patter—

All their sea sound
    the hum of who are
    partners of nothing.

O namer enamored of _____ .

    Ink-track a trick
Across that black
    & blank increase.

No agent, no object in
The white rites of what writes.

## 10.

If there is a Center it is not
     a pure point
     but a City
     empty of time.

Come, unmanned mind: enter Out.

Dis
     content of this
Thin
     king.

A species of space, a bird
Above unmoving masses.

Red word
Dead under
Deed: one

Series
Of one, shining vanishing.

Even—*raven*—odd.

# Q BED

*Of the doomed love between the sphere and the cube*: One who is radiance; one who is a section of night. One who is sole & whole; one who wears multiple, self-divisive faces. One as wide as the globe; the other collected into planar states. One whose spin brings peace; one whose spin violates space. One who speaks from a center; one who whispers in corners. One who is present to itself; one alien to its own aspects. All permission is round; all discipline demands a cutting. One a womb; the other a tomb.

# *TO THE THIRD POWER*

The cube is very stable upon the table.

The cube is the remnant of a perfect thought.

The vertices of the cube both control and conceal its power source.

The faces of the cube contain an innumerable swarm of points, ready to rebel against the eight privileged points that stand at its vertices.

The map of the cube shows an ocean at its center.

The cube is a continuation of chaos by other means.

Each face of the cube sees only its opposite as its mirror-self; as if ashamed, the other faces slant away in perspective.

The faces of the cube, the phases of the moon.

The cube is a box of eyes.

The cube is a six-legged insect trapped in abstraction.

The cube is the trumpet of an angular angel.

The point at the center of the cube incubates triangles.

The cube, as a closed system, is always cooler than its surroundings.

The cube is a garment dropped at the door of eternity.

The sex of the cube is the number six.

The cube, so rigid in all its relations, reeks of eros.

The brace of the cube is the embrace of pyramids.

The cube is a citadel standing at the end of history.

The cube wants only to rest here.

Nature does not want to make a cube.

The cube is a necessary accident; the cube is the wreckage of risk.

The cube is displayed before royalty as the last of its kind.

The cube is commanded into being, as formlessness laughs.

The cube, in order to be understood, must be floated in midair.

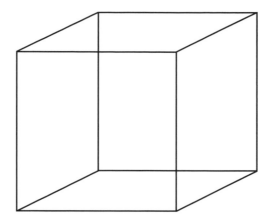

An old man walks into a cubical white room and notices his footprints reproduced on the ceiling above. He finds he cannot exit the room. As he paces, the pattern of his steps continues to be traced on the ceiling until it has been completely blackened. He stops and looks up into the pathless black. (Hint: there is a mathematical solution to his plight.)

# *DEFINE LION*

Hey hooded scholar: say *what,* say *why* or
Y-axis

—if today the sky is blue
It is

Unpossessed as any datum; so

Cold, culled
From all
        the fretted possibilities of blue.

        Uncalled, stand alone
Next to X.

~~To perceive is to unconceive.~~ Then
        to posit
A vacancy's born orb—

        so to say nothing
        of any man
Also monster, also star.

O sun, son of *sonnez,* I answer to
A mystery.

To posit without position—
  now-thing
  states, state
Enemy of my name.

"We" is then a wish away—

Bad history, bad witness: we be dust, the
  must of time.

# REVERSING RIVER

"The system is blinking red." That's what the man said.

Then what is stopping us? To arms, already!

Does the Revolution wait in words? Where do we find those (s)words?

Did the door dilate like an eye? Then what is located by the X of want, the Y of why?

I would argue that language allows the animal to jump out of its skin.

I would argue that information wants to be communist.

Dear maker, thy form = swarm.

*

But isn't the in-drawn, life-giving breath a silencing? And the expelled breath, necessary to voice, a rehearsal of the last breath?

Are we exiled into sound? No, call back the animal.

The shock of being human, as it passes through the body, is the shock of language.

# *ALARMIST*

O sick physick of the anti-sun!

When finality is the first
To say that

A
    light leads a-
    way, that
Nothing sources
    the blue in *blew*, the red in *bled*.

Blessed injury of the germ
    —its initial shine
A
    might of matter.

To spinning
    rage, its tangential—
To speech, each
Other.

Because cause cannot
    be *not*
    bent & rent—

On waking, the automaton can walk
    with breath re-
      verberant

Into the very data of the day.

# ONE BELOW BLESS

I bless *believing* as a Poverty.

I bless the Positive of *not* & *note*.

    Note: knit night.

Meet matter—more roar, more
Ash & thrash through time.

The part, the port—the winter of, the wanter of—

My said to seed, my read sidereal, one tear to tear.

    The ground is groaned: O
Red woman, what hue is man?

Cloud not alight not aloud—
    told
Cold union of I & I.

Object subject
    to the scrape of script, the claw of law.

We are, are we

a wake in the water of thought, a ware in the storehouse
of distance.

*The Dog Star is the nearest giant, & yet*
*a forgery of*
*God's lust & luster. A spiral is His suppressed ghost.*

Only lift left—so

bone cabinet, book & beaker.

Closed, the system dies. Open, it pretends to pray.

# BLIND ILLUMINATION

In one sense, infinitive
To phantom—
        I heard the room of all space, spinning.

What science
        guided me
Toward silence—
My wanting to know more about
        no more?

I wanted to hear about
The nothingness beyond God.

Stirred the random to render
Stored order—
        eye-dead I did.

Did I, within
        reason, reach
Toward the fluttering of my hands?

        To whom to answer, once
Flown alone to hymn?

Here, the noise in *soil* passes
For the pure O in *soul.*

No, touch
        can never touch
That which is
        composed of emptiness, of
        atoms.

So my flare-tipped fingers
        elongate into time.

# THE PHRASES
# OF THE MOON

## FULL

    The blow to a gong
—gone blind

    with the sight of white
Silk, O milk
    of my reason—

    sun reseen in
My mad mad mirror.

## GIBBOUS

Sense
Less science: the

Wish-apparition of a perfect fact.

    As thought, the war
Of one upon one.

## HALF

Half a mind almost mine.

Whole
       fragment, I am
A being from another word.


## CRESCENT

Bow bent back—to what release?

       My lone line, the join of all I am not.

A minor truth betrays
A major one—
A lore
       for the lyre.
For it is written: *liar* with a *why*.


## NEW

       Calling all coincidence, I will
Deem the dark my day.

Yet—if I say
    *I am lying,* I am lying
To you now.

O zero raised to zero—I am lying with you now.

# VOICE-OVER

*Is it a trick? The soundtrack is out of sync.*

In the spike of "speak," a spook.

All plural of I is Is, *pleurer.*

All plait of plaint is paint, a parent.

In the spirit of spit: the unsupported past.

As answer swerves & revs.

Met meat, meant mental for a furor—

A duel aloud in silence.

Before the assembled bled, I bled in fable.

\*

Unmake arrival, reversal. The risen smokes of a small universe.

That rival Mind will be winter, will be riven.


Rhyme of ice at the rim of time—laying

Earth atop earth—utopian birth—the play of plus minus us.

Any second must come before the first, for first is thirst:

la mer miroir, a pool loop. Here, hearer, no hero, no god is guide.


\*


To marrow, tomorrow.

To the numen of the new moon, O sole solar soul.


Élan, gauge language, thou able bubble, thou free & fragile jail!

But down & downer cannot be explained—

Nor the speed of the deeps, nor the Milk-splat of embodiment.


The site of I, a vertical gash.

Go ash. Begone, gown of flesh—


fled heart, red vegetable that winter leaves beliefless.

Will, at the trillionth hour, serves a bell-like power—

a truth table bare of all repast.


\*


No surer treasure than the trap of my ape-shadow.

Starting from the homonym of home—

My nature a frame in fracture.

Shall I then pose X, expose my star tissue?

Empirical to touch, the cost of empire—

What sound so wound, so round, so ruined?

# CALLING MISTER E

I have a message for Mister E that pertains to the poor, to the Invalid
as well. I have a message for Mister E to be delivered by a random walk.
*You are the twin of between, so resign your position, Mr. E.*

The center is the source of all violence, the eye's attempt at speech.

> Blue sky blew its skin, a night-cloak, a clock.
> Thought was blind, was ways & blaze of zero.

> Not to thank, is to think.
> Detonated, denotated. Mister E, we know your real identity.

Looking designs as it desires
—lacking coordinates, the eye turns inward, a spore's oratory of space.

So fact is Artifact, splayed resplendent.

*Now* the whole roll, the hole role, relic of the chase.
*Now* choicest estuary.
*Now* oldest newest.

A trick of the ink, or red electric lick, black blank.

Shy apparition, flaw is law—

ruling over the over-
flow of pure potential.

That violence touch the viol, and teach the air
The error of violet.

Saintly
light upon the rift, light upon the raft.

No, no
Star-swirl, all to all answering, all to all steering.

A
Dead
Dedicated to
Mister E

—author of A
World almost word.

# PROSE & PROSCENIUM

Kissed blackest, white awaits all on a bleak block.

One is too many in ideal order.
Seeming ardor, the most of missed.

No
Guard to regard, no netted night.

For all
      falls, fails, fools, feels—

As this space of spots
      stops time over
Breath's vibrato.

Red verses read, no re-
      verses no, being bang.

Between acts: the shadows
Stay alive, twist into the shapes of letters.

      It is said
They look like actors, reciting lines.
      *But to be what water, & what home to whom?*

# THE NEW EXPLANATIONS

A stern star, styling stilling—
A
    behavior of
        bad heaven—

We, as you
        is on a rocketship, yet risk
        I & I
On a yonder of red earth.

A
    shook system, the man
    around the woman, the

Cash of waves
    over cost.

Who the
Inhuman—

A
    look, a cycle of lack

Or
    the lore of mirror's mere aether.

*Explanation*: The killer of stone starts talking. The splinters displayed in evidence. *Inverse of earth: each answer to chime out of time.*

Utopian hurt the heart
Compiled unto polarity.

The taste of a tongue
Unto itself.

Leave out all reference, only
Leave alive.

*Explanation*: The many-eyed beast keeps looking into its own hand to locate the scene of terror. The error being to call, then to capitalize its name. *No answer.*

   Tell the die, hail
The body to be

No number than number—

Against the dark
   durance of its sound, *We*
Goes iridescent—
   word order under? over? world order—

all only
To object to object.

A

    single rebellious angle—

    bent nail
To hold together
    the god of hell.


*Explanation*: Effect of a posited mind-eye, perched on One / infinite
expenditure, else Nothing. *First fatality, or light exceptional to the shine
of night: a social good given for the right wrong answer.*


You, immune to motion, yet moan yes—

A

    dash, then sure erasure—

    the rest, wrest
    as sound asunder—No

    (the name of)
Shown
    (to mind alone)

In monotone of bone. Elemental lament.

No (turned
    inward) one
    body to be (to whom?) human—
A
    holy combustion
Become mirror-reversal. Here, its pose opposing

    Night's natal
Verses, versus
    (day undoing day)
    the first blurred word, the first blared
Hush.

*This*, the very word of
    this (heard
Hard) shared shard.

*Explanation*: To be beyond / needs to be thought, beyond / what needs
to be. The fiery fall, first iced, then twiced between time. *Real // answer
spliced.*

Go O: the sentience of the sentence, eating its own tail.
My guide, hide in-
    human.

Last animal circling back
To first person—the I closing
    upon its perfect form, bent (as if by consent) in two.

Being:
    the contract
Signed by an act of contraction.

So the social, destroyed, turns astronaut.

*Explanation*: To all the uncalled. Dome of order = the moral rind of random. If the letter A's parallel lines shall meet. Cold national ash, post notice. *Sum, answer sun.*

# ON REVISION

### 1.

Dear redeemer, or crossed-
    out choice: there are no crimes in nature.

    The thing is: A
Meaning wants an enemy.

Why light
Was made to miss—

Why the myth is little to the mouth.

### 2.

Trace, once traded for a deed, now dead:
A
Name too far from reference

    here returns to its ancestral treehouse.

    *See* Wood, knots in, 666; whorls in, 999.

**3.**

A
>     rampant temporality is needed—

>     one recursive to fire, uncontained
As any verb without a subject.

First never, first nerve—

The work of working *wing*
>     against *king*

>     to vary & to
Void its major meaning.

# THE ANSWER IS NO

Possessive of
    what
    whispering space—

No thought is thought: a ware aware
Of the value of air.

After yes, *Law's*
*Walls* falls, reason risen too heavy to heaven.

Here & here, the sore series rests—

    as thought without

    thing wears the ring.

# *UNFALL*

No, subtle sub-
    stance does not tend to settle—

A
    rest to wrest image & eye, mage
    of the stage of the stage of reason.

Cast origin, joker—

A law allows a lawless All
    to shame measure & mentation.

Never & again, the given.
Paren-
Thesis of ru(i)ne—

    of poorest
Rest our power—

*Violence seeks to escape the Law, yet
    it is an Imposition of the Law.*

Each to each, touch
    unchooses.

Ratchet &
    ratchet of real time.

Earth's reverse spin, love loveless but
    birdlike.

Real inside the spyglass:
    a single egret, sin-glow, regret.

Nature in its own Chase
    —the *alter* of the altar of

No offering, the fairest
Rest of fear.

# *THUNK*

Sun, shun real relation.

You (all)
Revoke, re-
    evoke my name.

Manner to man, I
    o'er error roar

Your ore & ire.

To escape a scape of eyes
    at all scales, untune Night.

A why, a wire we
Are.

Filling feeling

You
    think & thank
You.

Being
Being the one

    unstable, unstatable

    state—

*There*

    O

*Other*—a throw through aether.

# *THOUGHT THOU OUGHT*

Allow a low
    proportion—
    *eye : prism :: voice : prison.*


Sown, no—sewn, no—shown, no—


The line is blank.


Impure within imperative, the
    white sheet.


Lock out every
Interlocutor &


Let stay
The *stealth* in light, that
    *what*
    that won't, that
Want
In bluest visibility.


    Don't
Listen to the sun, its
    order roared to ardor—

O
Mass in its militancy, its melt—

Narrate
A ray or red area, an Aria to Time.
Teach each talk as stalk of all Star.

Starless, yet, the heart-stops of history—

a slow lottery, a slaughter. Other other—
Then
all dawn
comes down, a curtain

Too decadent, a pain-
painted Copy

too accurate to cure.

# NEITHER NOR

Silent, what
    listens, lists
Sideways—

Not & knot, knot &
Night—alight, a

Force
    paired
For a
    spared

Soul, sole
    respiring upward of
Word.

    All's spiral, as
    fall's Fall—finality's one
    line of flight—
    *fast, last.*

First the rest of
    fire's stay.
O stop
    step: one past

Opposite

    to posit

    what *went*: Eternal


    wait of one

For the other.

# NETHER ETHER

Not *not*:


Nature closed in that
Nature clothed in thought.


One from
    the other, both
    nether.


To the breather of ether


—the brooder
    on a frayed braid:


There
    *will be* a First.
There
    *was not* a Last.


U-
    nite night
To center
    said cinder, sad sender.

Time might mate (no matter).

Fire to lie, lie down before
    (a show of attrition) all truthful trees.

There
    the wear of *where*, attire-entire . . .

# *WHY TIME?*

*For David Meltzer*

Stand outside to know why.

Once, unknown noun, you had no need of the verb "to be" to be outside of time.

Nothing repeats, nothing is exact. To be exact, repeat your answer. A red letter, unread now, is curling through the air.

To appear (is) to be caught disappearing. That sentence (never to be stated) wants to advance into the future, but *now* is going the other way. *Now* can only vanish. You can't stay here.

Time is not a container, but a point of contact. Because you & I have names, we stand in the way of whatever wants to meet here.

In the old book, all or nothing has a name. Most names seem ciphers for suffering. But words desert their owners. Unless, until, we track them down in the desert.

What comes first partakes of nothing; therefore, if we can grasp anything, we can grasp only what comes second.

These letters fell out of time: *EIN SOF.*

The wine glass fell slowly to the floor & shattered—soundlessly. The spilled liquid immediately assumed the shape of the universe.

Truth of mind over matter: an ant crawling across a page of script.

Why time? Why this rhyme of *light* with *night,* of *first* with *thirst?*

What last will will *last* cast backward to *word?* Because no atom is alive, but accusative to being—

(R)endings, (m)endings: the job of legend. This (s)ending of—

This sounding of, the anti-angel.

Say, unsay, snake-wheel, O noose of Gnosis! Unlikely likeness: no eyes no yes.

Count chance's chants. To choose ruse as if to choose ruse.

# BACK OF

*(Being a sampling of "back-of" constructions
from Robert Duncan's* The H.D. Book*)*

Back of this world is the memory of another.

A mother back of Greece, back of America.

Back of the caprice, hysteria, fantasy—the psychic entity in men's minds of woman as all-powerful—and back of the other figure, the pure, higher, suffering Psyche-woman.

Back of the accusation against the Poet we find another accusation, against the psyche of woman.

I, too, believed that back of the army was a cult of war.

Back of such thought is a concept of universal sympathies, correspondences, communications.

Back of the sexual organs and the names.

Back of that civilization of meanings agreed-upon, that the dictionary represents.

Back of that old war between the Father and his hero-sons.

Back of Freud was the tradition of earlier Jewish mysticism.

Back of the later occultism, as back of the Freudianism of her middle period.

Back of the analysis room, his office, into his other room, his study.

And back of that home, the first home appears: it is the study of the father.

Back of what we knew as children, scenes were being shifted.

Back of these images of free wild elements in nature.

Back of the name I glimpse a fragment of the dream image.

Back of the later awakening of the man I was to be.

Back of this erotic replacement.

Back of these ideas as a recapitulation of primal experience.

Back of poetry, some collective poetic unconscious.

Not to find the fountain of feeling back of the poem.

Back of the stream-of-consciousness mode is Robert Browning's dramatic monologue.

Back of the famous rapture of H.D.'s early work.

Back of Bloom's personality is that of Odysseus.

Back of Greece, Egypt was primal, the depth to be sounded.

Back of, or below, the bird note of anguish.

As I found the Romantic spirit, and back of that, the spirit of Romance and back of that the cult of life as a romance of the spirit.

Not only may the past be back of the present, but the present may be back of the account of the past.

The source of the songs lies in an obscurity back of the first writing on the wall.

# THE PERSON

But, I have only ever seen The Person—my counterpart—against the grammatical background of interstellar night.

He stands at my door, little realizing the *zero* of predicate is one, while the *prey* of predicate is two. He will say only the errata: *red*, at war with itself; *blue,* always the last instance of blue.

The Person wears a headdress, a dress of thought.

The Person is male with female characteristics, fallen into autumns of stain & substance. His sin is a cinema of seeming, a body-sign of *both* & *neither* meeting, teeming.

The Person wears what is: a "melancholy cloud." My closed system.

His signs point backward. His eye wants what it cannot have.

Taste waste, the One without mouth, the Eye ever over I.

Icon of the blackness of Blankness, icon of the whiteness of Witness.

Cite I, seer: O deafened hour, defend ear.

My, my, cold, cold, pyre a poor evaluator, & "alive" a lottery of lit particulars.

Because the sun dies in eyes, day is all Idea: a phosphorescent night-scape of skin & bone.

The start of art is always too soon or too late. My statement corrected, as sonically connected, gives only what cannot *not* be given: the empty set, once pieced together; the ware of whereness once aware.

Depart, part: pay per sun; pay per perishing, shadow—

## *A* = *A*

Mine to ask a mask to say, A is not A.

No one, ever the contrarian, to answer.

The moon is both divided & multiplied
    by water: as chance, as the plural of chant.

O diver, to be sea-surrounded by a thought bled white—
    a blankness as likely as blackness.

What is the word for getting words & forgetting?

Might night right sight?

I, too late to relate
    I & I, trap light in sound
& sing no thing that breath can bring.

Andrew Joron's previous books of poetry include *Trance Archive: New and Selected Poems* (City Lights, 2010), *The Sound Mirror* (Flood Editions, 2008), *Fathom* (Black Square Editions, 2003), and *The Removes* (Hard Press, 1999). He has also published two volumes of prose: *The Cry at Zero* (Counterpath Press, 2007), a selection of prose poems and critical essays, and *The Sun at Night* (Black Square Editions, 2004), a survey of American surrealist poetry. From the German, he has translated *The Perpetual Motion Machine* by the proto-Dada fantasist Paul Scheerbart (Wakefield Press, 2011) and the *Literary Essays* of Marxist-Utopian philosopher Ernst Bloch (Stanford University Press, 1998). As a musician, Joron plays the theremin in various experimental and free-jazz ensembles. He teaches creative writing at San Francisco State University.